MW01127294

Jehoshaphat

2 Chronicles 20:1–30

Story by Gail Pawlitz
Illustrated by James Watling

Copyright © 2005 Concordia Publishing House
3558 S. Jefferson Avenue, St. Louis, MO 63118-3968
1-800-325-3040 • www.cph.org

This publication may be available in braille, in large print, or on cassette tape for the visually impaired. Please allow 8 to 12 weeks for delivery. Write to the Library for the Blind, 7550 Watson Rd., St. Louis, MO 63119-4409; call 1-888-215-2455; or visit the Web site www.blindmission.org

Manufactured in Colombia

1 2 3 4 5 6 7 8 9 10   14 13 12 11 10 09 08 07 06 05

Men rushed into the great hall. They had bad news
for the king.

"Good king, Jehoshaphat," they said. "A large and
mighty enemy is coming near. We fear a mighty battle."

The king looked worried. He said, "Gather my people. We must go without eating to show our sorrow. We must pray. We need help from the Lord."

People came from all over the kingdom. They hurried to the temple-church.

Jehoshaphat stood in the courtyard before the people and prayed to God. He asked God to save

the people from the power of the mighty enemy.

"Please, Lord," Jehoshaphat prayed. "Tell us
what to do for we are very weak. Help us! Save us
by Your might!"

God heard the prayers. Jahaziel was able to tell the people God's answer.

"Do not worry," God said. "The battle is Mine. Tomorrow you must come and see how I will save you!"

Jehoshaphat and the people were so happy that God would fight for them. They fell down before the Lord and gave thanks. They sang loud, joyful songs because the battle was the Lord's.

Early the next morning, Jehoshaphat led the people south. They marched out to the wilderness to see how God would win. Jehoshaphat said, "Believe God's words.

Believe that the Lord is with you. God will save you."
The people marched. The people believed.
The people sang, "Praise the Lord. His love never ends."

While the people were marching and singing, God was at work. The almighty Lord set an ambush. The enemy troops were tricked into fighting one another until no one was left alive. The mighty army wasn't so mighty anymore.

When the battle was over, God's people picked up clothing and riches left behind. After three days, they praised God and prepared to go home.

Jehoshaphat led the joyful crowd all the way back to Jerusalem. On the way, they played harps and blew trumpets. The almighty God had defeated their enemies.

When the crowd reached the city, they went to the temple-church. They prayed and gave thanks. They sang, "Praise the Lord. His love never ends."

What wonderful news! God has defeated our enemies too! Like Jehoshaphat and the people of Judah, we gather in church to rejoice. There we pray, we praise, and we give thanks.

God sent His only Son, Jesus, to fight a battle we could not win. He died on the cross to defeat our worst enemies: sin, death, and the devil. Now, through Baptism and His Word, we receive God's gifts of forgiveness and life everlasting.

Word Matching Game

Now that you've learned about Jehoshaphat, you can play this matching game. Draw a line with your finger from the picture to the word it goes with.

prayer

forgiveness

temple

king

trumpet

"Praise the Lord. His love never ends."
He is strong enough to help
us in any trouble.